CONSTRUCTION MACHINES!
Dig it! Move it! Dump it! Build it!

Written by C.J. McDonald

**Designed by Daniel Jankowski
and Bill Henderson**

Copyright © 2019 Scholastic Inc.

Tangerine Press
an imprint of
SCHOLASTIC
scholastic.com

Scholastic, Tangerine Press, and associated logos are trademarks and/or registered trademarks of Scholastic Inc.

Published by Tangerine Press,
an imprint of Scholastic Inc.,
557 Broadway, New York, NY 10012

10 9 8 7 6 5 4 3 2 1

ISBN: 978-1-338-31976-7

Printed in Changsha City, China
Construction vehicle made in
Shantou, China

Table of Contents

Machines at Work!

Construction machines—operated by a driver inside a **cab**—clear land, dig **foundations** and **trenches,** move and lift waste and heavy building **materials,** and help build roads and sidewalks. Let's get to know some of the hardest-working construction vehicles on the planet!

Move It!

Movers carry heavy loads like rock, dirt, and building materials—and sometimes other work machines!

Build It!

Some construction machines mix and pour materials for building roads, sidewalks, and foundations. Others make sure the material is laid right so the building, sidewalk, or road will be safe.

Dump It!

Dump trucks keep construction projects moving by carrying materials to and from job sites.

Dig It!

Diggers can have buckets, drills, or shovels. Some diggers dig smaller holes, but others can dig really deep ones!

Dirt-Loving Diggers

These tough work machines aren't afraid to get dirty. In fact, they're made for it! Diggers—using their shovels, buckets, drills, or chains—are needed at every construction job. Without diggers, we wouldn't have foundations, basements, underground utilities, tunnels, or **pilings** for bridges.

DIG IT!

Dirt-Loving Diggers

Diggers with Shovels

Loaders can't dig deep, but they can dig and move large amounts of dirt and rock in one big scoop!

Diggers with Drills

Some machines **bore** through rock to make tunnels for mining or for cars and trucks.

Diggers with Chains

Chained diggers can create deep ditches where power lines, pipes, or cables can be safely buried.

Diggers with Buckets

These earthmoving diggers can go deep into the ground and scoop up big loads. Some are strong enough to break through rock!

Backhoes

The backhoe is part tractor, part loader, and part excavator. The driver can use the loader shovel at one end to dig small holes, clear land, or move material. The bucket attached to the flexible arm at the other end of the cab can dig deeper holes. The different diggers are usually only used one at a time so the machine doesn't fall over.

DIG DEEPER

The backhoe is one of the most popular machines on a construction site because it can do many jobs and moves around easily.

Excavators

Excavators dig deep holes—fast! But like many work machines, excavators do more than just dig. They can pull trees out of the ground or slam their buckets against buildings to knock them down. They can also move or load dirt or rock.

DIG DEEPER

The world's largest excavator is as tall as a three-story building!

DIG DEEPER

Mini excavators can move around in tight spaces, such as backyards, where they could be used to dig the ground for pools.

Loaders

With sturdy wheels and large shovels, loaders handle big jobs at construction sites. Loaders can dig holes, clear roads, and lift or move anything including construction waste, logs, animal feed, rocks, and other materials. They use their shovels to dump their loads into trucks that carry the loads away.

Different types of loaders are needed for different jobs. The arm linked to the shovel of a swing loader moves from side to side, making it useful in smaller spaces. Some skid-steer loaders and wheel loaders can be outfitted with forks or even brooms so they can do even more jobs.

DIG DEEPER

Meet the world's largest wheel loader. It can lift the weight of six elephants!

Pile Drivers

Have you ever heard loud **booms** near a construction project? You might have heard a pile driver, which drives pilings deep into the ground to hold up the buildings, bridges, and other structures.

Workers usually use noisy pile drivers during the day, when most people are awake.

DIG DEEPER

Pile drivers are often used to drive pilings into seabeds to build piers, bridges, or wind farms, or to help reach natural gas and oil buried deep within the ocean floor.

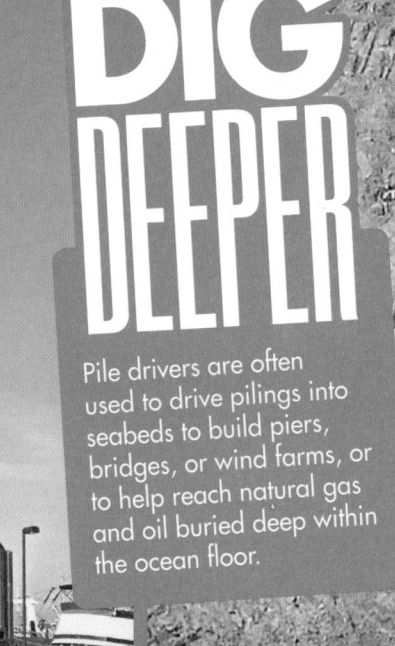

Tunnel Boring Machines

Have you ever seen a mole hole in your yard? Moles are expert tunnel builders. That's why tunnel boring machines (TBMs) are also called moles. These big machines chew through rock using round cutters.

DIG DEEPER

Thanks to giant TBMs, people can travel through a tunnel that goes under the English Channel between England to France in just 20 minutes!

Road Headers

Construction machines do big jobs and often make big messes. But some road headers—another type of boring machine—actually clean up after themselves! They can even spray jets of water to get rid of the dust in the air as they drill.

Trenchers

To lay pipes, power lines, or utility cables, you need a trencher. This machine digs long, narrow ditches called trenches. To do the job, trenchers are equipped with long, toothed metal wheels or chains that can cut through everything from soft dirt to **pavement**.

DIG DEEPER

Trenches have a long history in warfare. Soldiers hide inside them while defending themselves.

Dirt-Loving Diggers Fact

Hammers can be attached to excavators to help them break through rock.

Mighty Movers

What do movers move? Everything! They clear dirt, rock, and waste out of the way. They lift materials and even workers into place. They **transport** supplies and other construction vehicles to and from job sites. And when their fellow work machines stir up too much dust, they carry in water to help keep dirt under control.

MOVE IT!

Mighty Movers

Movers That Transport!

Some movers transport construction machines and supplies over roads and highways to construction sites.

Movers That Carry!

Some movers carry heavy loads of materials such as dirt, rock, or **mineral**s across construction sites.

Movers That Remove!

Some movers don't just move. They *remove!* They can push away heavy loads of dirt and rock or even push buildings down!

Movers That Lift!

Some movers can be seen rising above tall buildings. Others can lift and carry loads around worksites.

Crawler Loaders

Part tractor and part front loader, crawler loaders have tracks, giving them the ability to handle all types of **terrain** and move about on job sites. Their wide tracks help them stay put even on soft ground, making them useful in building roads, construction, and clearing land.

"It looks like a caterpillar!" said a man who looked at a picture of an early crawler loader. The company that made it became known as the Caterpillar Tractor Co., which is one of the world's largest makers of construction machines.

DIG DEEPER

Tractors

When we think of tractors, we often think of farms. But tractors also work hard on construction sites, where they can push and pull loads or act as diggers using shovels and buckets.

DIG DEEPER

Tractors can be wheeled and tracked. Tracked tractors can make tight turns and can easily go up hills.

Bulldozers

For pushing, moving, wrecking, spreading, and even digging, the mighty bulldozer is the go-to work machine. Bulldozers run on tracks and have large metal **blades** or plates at the front. The blades can tilt or move up or down.

DIG DEEPER

Bulldozers can do many jobs— including making art. Workers at a Japanese festival used bulldozers to help create a giant snow sculpture.

DIG DEEPER

Inside their cabins, bulldozer drivers can sit in air-conditioning while doing hard work.

Scrapers

When you're driving along a smooth road, you can thank a scraper—at least in part. Scrapers are important in road and highway construction. A blade at the bottom scrapes away the top layer of earth and dumps it into a giant bowl. When the bowl is full, the dirt is carried away.

DIG DEEPER

The first scrapers were made of wood and were pulled by horses. Tractors later replaced horses.

Conveyors

When you go to the grocery store, you put your groceries on a belt that moves them toward the cash register. That belt is called a conveyor. Now imagine a giant conveyor that can move heavy or **bulky** material across construction sites!

DIG DEEPER

The world's largest conveyor is so big it can be seen from space!

Cranes

Meet some of the heavy lifters of any construction site! Sometimes towering high above the skyline, cranes use **pulleys** and cables to lift, move, and lower heavy objects such as steel beams and other heavy materials used for building. Their long arms can get into hard-to-reach areas.

DIG DEEPER

A pulley helps you lift more with less work using a rope or cord that wraps around a wheel. The more pulleys you use, the lighter the load seems!

Forklifts

Using their pronged platforms, forklifts can raise, lower, and move materials at construction sites. They are also used for icky jobs—dumping garbage into bins or carrying portable toilets.

DIG DEEPER

Forklifts can be equipped with booms so they can be used as cranes, or even with plows so they can clear away dirt and snow.

Hoists

When working on tall buildings, workers need a safe way to lift heavy materials, tools, and workers to upper levels. The answer is a hoist. Hoists can look like elevators, platforms, or like a little of both.

DIG DEEPER

Like cranes, hoists use pulleys to help do all that heavy lifting.

Water Trucks

Water trucks help builders fight dust and the risk of fire. They also help pack down soil, and are often used in mining and drilling. They can carry tens of thousands of gallons (or liters) of water to control dust clouds created when moving large amounts of dirt.

DIG DEEPER

When builders work in dry areas, such as deserts or places where there is a **drought**, they use water trucks to control the dust, which can cause air **pollution**.

Flatbed Trailer Trucks

All those heavy construction machines and building materials don't travel to worksites by themselves. They have to be hauled to the site on flatbed trailers, huge trucks capable of carrying really heavy loads.

Truckers go through special training to learn to handle their big **rigs**. They need a lot more time to come to a stop, and they have to make much wider turns than other vehicles.

DIG DEEPER

Mighty Movers Fact

Crawler loaders are often hard at work carrying and spreading waste around landfills. Talk about a stinky job!

Dumpers

No construction site would be complete without dump trucks! Dump trucks move materials to or around work areas or carry away waste from the site. And with dumpers, the bigger, the better! Bigger trucks mean fewer trips back and forth.

DUMP IT!

Dumpers

Big, Bigger, Biggest!
Dumpers are rated by how much they can carry. Most dump trucks used in construction can carry about 108 wheelbarrows full of dirt, rock, or other material!

Work Buddies
Dump trucks have to work side by side with construction machines like excavators, which lift and drop their loads right into the back of the truck.

Rolling Along
Dump trucks can have as few as six tires or as many as 22. Some have extra wheels that can be lowered when the truck is carrying a heavy load.

Standard Dump Trucks

When you think of dump trucks, you probably picture the standard dump truck. Usually having either six or 10 wheels, the truck dumps its load using a lift between the cab and the body. The driver uses a **lever** in the cab to control the dumper.

DIG DEEPER

Dumpers use **gravity** to help their tippers dump their loads.

Off-Road Dump Trucks

You'll often see standard dump trucks on the highway, but you'll only find off-road dump trucks on worksites, especially at mines. These trucks are made for rough terrain! Plus these dumpers can take tight turns despite their size.

DIG DEEPER

Off-roaders are built tough and strong. Many of these special dumpers are so big that they have to be built at the job site!

Side Dumpers

Trucks that dump from their ends are also known as tippers for a very good reason: they're prone to tip over. However, side dumpers—trucks that empty from their sides—are less likely to tip. They dump dirt or rock in long rows.

DIG DEEPER

The openings—or gates—of side dumpers can be twice as wide as those of end dumpers. This means side dumpers can't carry as much but can be emptied and filled faster.

The World's Largest Dump Trucks

These giant dumpers deserve some respect! They are powerful, hard-working hauling machines that can be longer than two buses parked end to end!

The Liebherr T 282B

Standing even taller than the Komatsu 930E, the Liebherr T 282B can carry the weight of 200 family cars! The driver climbs a tall ladder just to get into the cab!

The Caterpillar 797B

Once known as the world's largest dump truck, the Caterpillar 797B is still a mighty mining machine able to carry huge amounts of copper, coal, gold, and iron ore.

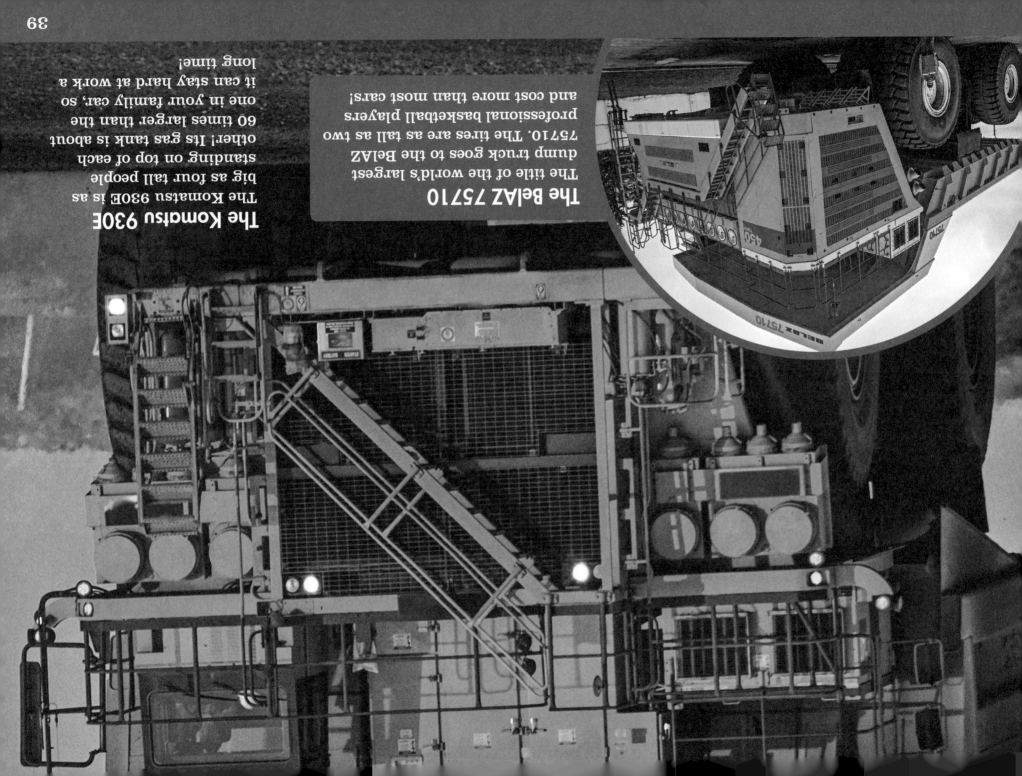

The Komatsu 930E

The Komatsu 930E is as big as four tall people standing on top of each other! Its gas tank is about 60 times larger than the one in your family car, so it can stay hard at work a long time!

The BelAZ 75710

The title of the world's largest dump truck goes to the BelAZ 75710. The tires are as tall as two professional basketball players and cost more than most cars!

Dumpers Fact

The design of standard dump trucks helps them move easily around construction sites. But they can't work on soft ground. That's a job for an off-road dumper!

Compactors, Mixers, and Pavers

Compactors, mixers, and pavers prepare the materials that become our roads, sidewalks, driveways, bike paths, and foundations of homes and buildings of all types.

BUILD IT!

Compactors, Mixers, and Pavers

Made for the Grade

Graders team up with other work machines like bulldozers to spread dirt brought in dump trucks. This will help support a road that will be built over it.

From the Ground Up

Once the dirt is laid, the road needs a smooth and even foundation. This is a job for compactors!

The Perfect Mix

When the road is ready for paving, concrete or **asphalt** mixers bring in the wet material that becomes the road's surface.

Hit the Road

Pavers spread out the concrete or asphalt in an even layer. Soon the road will be ready for traffic!

Compactors

Have you ever seen a crack in a sidewalk or road? Chances are the ground under it wasn't compacted—or packed down—the right way. Compactors pack ground hard so it can hold up under traffic. They also pack down dirt under the foundations of homes and other buildings so they will stay strong and dry.

DIG DEEPER

To choose what type of compactor to use, builders have to test the soil. Some soils contain sand and gravel. Other soils contain clay and finer grains called silt.

Concrete Mixers

Concrete mixers are important because much of our world is built using concrete. Concrete is strong, safe, and it saves energy by helping buildings stay cool.

DIG DEEPER

The spinning drums inside concrete mixers keep the concrete from hardening till it is poured.

DIG DEEPER

Dump trucks pour asphalt into a paver's **hopper**. The asphalt is then carried to the back of the paver on a conveyor to be spread on the ground.

Like many work machines, concrete pavers do many jobs. They spread the concrete that will form the road or foundation. They shake the concrete to fill in air bubbles. Then they push the larger pieces of the concrete to the surface to make it even stronger.

Pavers

Graders

Before the compactor gets to the scene, a grader has already been hard at work to level the ground. The long blade at the bottom makes the ground wide, smooth, and flat for roads or foundations.

DIG DEEPER

Graders can sometimes double as snowplows, so a grader may be the machine that makes sure you can get to school after a snowstorm. Sorry, kids!

When compactors, mixers, and pavers do their jobs right, our buildings, roads, and sidewalks will serve us well for many years.

Glossary

Asphalt a mixture of materials known by its dark color and used to pave roads and other surfaces

Blade flat edge used for digging

Boom a long beam used to hold or move heavy objects

Bore to make a hole in something

Bulky taking up much space, possibly making it hard to move

Cab the compartment where a driver sits while driving a construction vehicle

Drought dry conditions from a long amount of time without rain

Foundation the base of a building, often found underground

Gravity the force that draws objects and people to the ground

Hopper a large container that holds material and releases it from the bottom

Lever a handle used to control a machine

Lever

Asphalt

Glossary

Material supplies needed for an activity—in this case, construction

Mineral a hard material from which rocks, including coal and gems are made, which is found in nature and is not made of living things

Pavement a surface paved with rock, concrete, or asphalt

Piling strong stakes or posts that support a large structure

Pollution harmful substances or particles that hurt the environment

Pulley a wheel with a rope or cord used to lift heavy weights

Rig another word for truck

Site the ground on which something is built

Terrain a stretch of land known for its features, such as hills or flatness

Transport to take people or materials from one place to another using a vehicle of some sort

Trench a long, narrow ditch often used for burying power lines, pipes, and cables

Trench